MARYS OF THE SEA
JOANNA C. VALENTE

the operating system
brooklyn ny

the operating system print//document

MARYS OF THE SEA

ISBN 978-1-946031-08-2
Library of Congress Control Number 2017908559

copyright © 2017 by Joanna C. Valente
cover design by Lynne DeSilva-Johnson from original art by Ted Chevalier

edited and designed by Lynne DeSilva-Johnson

is released under a Creative Commons CC-BY-NC-ND
(Attribution, Non Commercial, No Derivatives) License:
its reproduction is encouraged for those who otherwise could not afford its purchase in the case of academic, personal, and other creative usage from which no profit will accrue. Complete rules and restrictions are available at: http://creativecommons.org/licenses/by-nc-nd/3.0/

For additional questions regarding reproduction, quotation, or to request a pdf for review contact **operator@theoperatingsystem.org**

This text was set in Odalisque, Minion, Franchise, and OCR-A Standard, printed and bound by Spencer Printing, In Honesdale, PA, in the USA. Books from The Operating System are distributed to the trade by SPD, with ePub and POD via Ingram.

*Second / Expanded Edition. Original printing by ELJ Editions, 2016.

the operating system
141 Spencer Street #203
Brooklyn, NY 11205
www.theoperatingsystem.org
operator@theoperatingsystem.org

MARYS OF THE SEA
JOANNA C. VALENTE

ACKNOWLEDGEMENTS & GRATITUDE

Endless thanks & eternal love to Monica Ferrell, Dennis Nurkse, Cathy Park Hong, Marie Howe, Rachel Eliza Griffiths, Stephen O'Connor, Stephanie Valente, Ted Chevalier, Lisa Marie Basile, Michael Seidlinger, Lynne Desilva-Johnson, Anthony Cappo, Gregory Crosby, Abigail Welhouse, Oren Misholy, Sean H. Doyle, Chris Antzoulis, Monica Lewis, Cameron DeOrdio, Marcus Bowers, Joseph Richard Izzo, Jason Koo, Lucas Hunt, Jonathan Papernick, Leah Umanksy, Shamar Hill, Joseph Quintela, John Maher, Fox Frazier-Foley, Hannah Lee Jones, David Tomas Martinez, Nathan McClain, Molly Tolsky, and to all of my friends and family who I love with all my heart.

Thank you to the publications who have featured versions of these poems:

The 22 Magazine, decomP, Drunk in a Midnight Choir, Italics Mine, La Fovea, Literary Orphans, Lyre Lyre, North Chicago Review, The Paris-American, Public Pool, Primal School, Steam Ticket, Souvenir Lit Journal, The Submission, Tipton Poetry Journal, Thrush Poetry Journal, The Tulane Review, Women Arts Quarterly, The Writing Disorder, The Write Room, Moonsick Magazine, PANK, & Apogee.

For Ted

CONTENTS

The Only Way Inside is Through the Back Door	11
Twin Lovers	12
American Express	13
Pandora Unborn	14
Their Hell	15
Creation Myth	17
Birth of Dionysus	19
Threshold	20
Toil & Trouble	21
The Formation of a Black Hole	22
Mythos	24
A Disease Called the Virgin	25
Fool's Wild	28
They Taught Us How to Be Wives	29
The Universe Is an Empty Gin Bottle	30
When We Were Born, We Did Not Live	31
In the Beginning, Everything Was Water	32
La Llorona	34
Family Moon	35
Heartstrings	36
Bainbridge Avenue	38
The Devil's Wedding	39
United States of Blood	40
Mary & Joseph Build a House Under the Brooklyn Bridge	41
You're Only Human When Someone is Looking	42
Poems are Written By Adults Who Have Killed Their Mothers	43
Siren Song	44
World Myth Parent	45
Scientists Discover How to Eliminate Emotion	47

Mary Said	48
Saturn Return	49
We Sleep with Dead People	50
Your Only Son is Dead	51
Magic Hour	52
The Art of Disappearing Is Hard to Master	53
The Pill Versus the Springhill Mine Disaster	54
Only Assholes Live in Brooklyn	55
Mittleschmerz	56
My Taste in Men Started Young	57
In the Future, Everyone Will Forget What They Look Like	58
Marys of the Sea	59
There Is No G[od] Train Running	63
The Universe Sends Its Condolences	64
Removal of Heart Artillery	65
Is It the Afterlife Yet?	66
Earth at the Time of Mercury Retrograde	68
Everyone You Love Has Been Found Dead	70
Phenomenology	71
Children of Paradise (Lost)	72
Lullaby on the Half Shell	73
Negative Space	74
Death Mask	75
Who Are You and Whom Do You Love	76
Assume the Position	77
Tarot Reading	79
Poetics and Process	81

"Have pity on those who are separated from someone they love.
Have pity on the loneliness of our hearts...

...And the soul asked, why do you judge me,
although I have not judged?

The soul answered and said, I saw you.
You did not see me nor recognize me.
I served you as a garment and you did not know me."

-Gospel of Mary-

THE ONLY WAY INSIDE IS
THROUGH THE BACK DOOR

i.
All mothers eat their children. All children drink their mothers.
My mother is grass growing from the underside of a rock,
hair tucked away from her face except for one strand,
constantly falling when she talks about hiring a new babysitter.
Her body no longer holds the many possibilities ahead
before the children.

One day, I had come home from school knowing there
was a sickness in my gut. When the doctor asked me where
it hurt, I pointed. Bury it in the soil, he instructed—there was no
chance unknowing. Dying children are only getting lonelier.
No one likes children but that doesn't mean you don't
have them.

ii.

Something's coming out of my ears—ink or shadow?
I can't make it stop. A little blue bird is fluttering around inside
my brain, plucking out memories until my post-nasal drip
is white noise.

In Sunday school, love was taught like blueberries
baking in crust: let simmer & don't eat it all at once.
I always ate too much until my plate emptied. I don't want
to go, but I am alone in this feeling. Left to carry it gracefully
until I'm alive in someone else's memory.

TWIN LOVERS

        Mercury comes down

            lady & lord move

                in mind's eye the spell fly

within their rebellion

      all nights neither dark

nor black only fig trees

            silhouetted against headless

              statues where birds build

                nests & Mary's body

                  pregnant
                  shapeless face

              finding roots in devil's
              pool—

        each one stretches them

AMERICAN EXPRESS

It was a pill
that shifted you
from my womb
to homeless:
transfer credit acct
to debit / type in data
& print out confirmation
of empty uterus.

So early you're hardly
alive / not even considered
'baby' but 'parasite'
—this is what I have told
myself & your father
& mostly I believe it—
not baby but parasite
as in tapeworm as in
flesh eating bacteria
as in child support bills
as in a love I cannot
charge.

Ten years from now
a transfer will occur
from debit acct
to my credit.
I hope it will be you
no longer lost
on the streets of
Not Ready Yet.

PANDORA UNBORN

Water in we / waved gigantic from shells / lost a home
found woman / turned her into a bird / cawed her listen
/ every Halloween her feathers turn white / until May
colors them / her daddy on the road

uses GPS to find him /has better luck debating
the wind / her mama gave birth / stillborn / says *come
to me apocalypse* / says *love me wild as atoms* /just when
the crazy's out / it gets let back in / all years pass—

THEIR HELL

Lucifer peeled her
                                    an orange, fed her girl-mouth
            kept strangers away.
                                    Some things he could give.
There were blue jays.
                        He birthed them for her
                                        barely made the
subway home.

               An old woman slept
                                on his shoulder, gathering

                                  ruin.

He loved these children—
                            his shadow wives.

                       Only during mercury retrograde
   under a shut-off moon would he bring
                               newcomers as tribute,

          kept dark

                 distant from her bedroom.
                           Grew azaleas & wisteria inside
   her bookcase, fastened Christmas

                         lights around the canopy.

                        Mary loved his pocket watch
                                            its bone fingers would skip
                    like a record, remind her
                                        of hurricanes taking whole

                cities as tribute , shredding pulses
                                    like packages. Lucifer came back
        with the clipped wings
                                        of a dove, her lover

                        climbed on top of her
                                        a candle in each hand.
    Left in a room of her own
                                    she mourned her mother's

                                    belly, brewed a fear
            that she loved a void.

CREATION MYTH

You ask me why I never pressed
charges. I drink the rest of my gin & tonic,
begin to tell you how a man

discovered eternal life in 1988. He found
it on the ocean floor. Instead of dying,
jellyfish age in reverse—bury themselves

until tiny flecks rise in gleams, endlessly
rocking. An injured medusa will sink
& reabsorb into the ocean floor—

it will wait. Eventually, a polyp will form
to reproduce a medusa. The easiest way
to make a jellyfish regenerate

is to mutilate it. It does not feel when
attacked. Someday I won't feel anymore
either. We both play dumb

when the bartender asks if we're okay
—I rock my chair the way a mother rocks
her child—ocean rocking a sailboat in arms

of salt. Self-control is difficult for humans:
our hearts still primitive. I scratch at skin
until a new layer reveals

impermeable. In the dim light of the bar,
all the bodies so dense, pores secreting
black. They almost disappear.

When it's time, you ask my name. Look
for J's—you'll find them everywhere:
24 hour diners, cliffside harbors in low

sunlight—hotel rooms with unsure
women. I was there once, in a room with
a man. It was late-winter in a big city

where lights no longer cared about sounds
during sex. He taught me how to keep my body
still & thin as pine needles, how to listen

to Billie Holiday cry in the backseat
of my car, how to take a pill so a child dies—
how every spring, fewer azaleas stay

in bloom. I smelled my cunt souring,
something gone wrong—violence never
far from the hands of men:

hands around neck—my life still believing
in the yet-to-be. The future has changed.
Early bloomer, still waiting for the one poem

that will bring me home. I didn't tell you how
I used to think of all the ways to fall in front
of cars, sacrifice my body to get what I had

before. I used to pray for a new body by moon
light, a return to being human. I leave without giving
you my name. I do not believe in punishment.

BIRTH OF DIONYSUS

lion jumps / through elephant craniums / fire whizzes moss-ravaged
jaws / jade clouds seam dawn / someone forgot to close
the gate / his mother is alone / mostly on knees curling plumed
serpents / around black fog / day-moon eclipses
her womb / into a book of names

THRESHOLD

Something fell on Lincoln Ave / Mammoth teeth
in rock salt in lime in a whale's belly / a wooden
chair breaks under weight /

Paid $25 for avocado n' fish n' yucca n' lemons
to feed humans saying / *lonely let me be*
when the tonality shifts / it is easier to be
evasive than to tell any truth /

& lack of truth can be blamed on brokeness
2 yrs ago was 2 yrs ago / not unremembered
in teeth / in tonal changes / over

landmasses, sea-stuff / Still I carry his name
in my cervix / at night peeling my eyes like onion
skinning off lost papers / they disappear /

hope they disappear / Cannot dream anything
in color except scribbled words (who's biography?) /
red ink that writes *don't let me be*

TOIL & TROUBLE

Stirring the pot, I mix poppy seeds, almond extract,
goldenseal & lime in mud—it's somebody
else's will. Three times a day

on an empty stomach—or soon to be empty—I avoid
the living, allowing hands

of dead children to coil my uterus—working their magic.
Even now, I taste the skin of their fingers, bitter creatures.

THE FORMATION OF
A BLACK HOLE

    i.

                        My lover & I need
        to cross a bridge.
                                   It is chained closed
            for the night.

                  My lover
                              climbs over
          leaves me

                              to hunt antelope
      distinguish poison

                                       from sustenance
   X marks the X.
                  I take a piece
                      of charcoal & draw
until my body

                              is covered

    ii

            Found dead   my lover
                is stolen   hooked
            up to machines—
                           his tongue pickled
            in salt   extracting
                  new blessings.
                                    It says do not
            tempt

iii

                                                                                    My lover still
                   —us unfound   his
                                         particles move
        in mephitic air.

                  My lover is
                              a hypernova.
                 I cut
                         apple skins
                                                   pour
                                                               2%
milk into
                          a jug—any size—keep
       pouring until
                 it sucks my vulva outside

                 until he screams on the other side
                                               of the house,

            the hummingbirds are gone.

MYTHOS

Billowing pelicans & car exhaust
echo on wild—a threshold of sky
twilights, preserved in canisters.

At midnight, he will hatch—
skin sack of moth larva.

You will pray to bargain
his soul for yours.

A DISEASE CALLED THE VIRGIN

i.

                          The Virgin walks into a bar

orders scotch

              & says *I took a man*
home last night

              I think He's dead

He never woke up.

ii.

     The Virgin walks

              into a bar   says *someone*

                    please take me home

                    but don't love me

        He made that mistake once

                      it killed Him.

iii.

                                            The Virgin walks into

               a bar & says

                             I wanted to marry a poet
        so I wouldn't have   *a green lawn*
like everyone else

                                   orders a rum
            & coke

                              everyone is asleep but Him

         soaks her fingers
                in whiskey, touches

         then generations come

                        then a pulse, His pulse.

iv.

                    The Virgin
                                walks into a bar
sits on a stool & says

         So this is the new world
                                    still
                      king deep

still making love

between a meat grinder
& a man's corpse, all the women in her still
& tired, all the women

tired inside her.

v.

Someone at the bar wakes up   walks over

to The Virgin

scrapes together two stones.

FOOL'S WILD

i.

Circle of bees humming
in my womb / circle of spiders
crafting webs over & over
after rain railroads
each thread. Before you
were born, you let out
a cry—

on the walls of my uterus
you wrote about a young poet's
fingerprints—behind my back
yours have been watermarked.

In other languages my heart
beats us both alive, wedges
between words I speak, creating
silence to hold a dead child, running
across the Pacific from Seoul—

ii.

We share the same waters
baby girl / try my eyes:
take them out nicely—
don't scrape too hard around.
In the open, I'll ask you
to stuff papers with the word
slut on the inside.

Losing streak, home destroyed
itself. Gonna drown / lonely passed
from generation to generation.

THEY TAUGHT US HOW TO BE WIVES

                                        I came home with you
            walked under rain all windows
                      open urgent as sirens
                              —silverfish in water beneath

     kitchen sink   street poets
                      speak merengue—speak out
   of tune

                 no
   squeeze goat brains
                        into ice pitcher & drink

                                'til death blows out of body
            trumpets your desire for body
     for anybody   you blow smoke
                  in return

[Year of the dragon

     born I
           —a temptation

small hourglass   no pearls cultured
    out-of-print journal   blue topaz
             set in 18k
the price

                    named for God's grace
          the virgin whose uterus
              was left behind in a baby grand
     piano which holds
               a dial phone used for sex
    which is now legally a comet ;;;

          who finally learned how
                   to say please]

THE END OF THE UNIVERSE IS AN EMPTY GIN BOTTLE

        all animals but one
            closeted in black holes
                across space; before living
                    I was *we*, canoeing
                          around the rings of Saturn
                              then fell into

                              life to rise out atoms
                      ripped apart one-by-one;
              summon your body
        of performance.

WHEN WE WERE BORN, WE DID NOT LIVE

A hole in space ran naked,
like deer across stretches of road

stopping only for high-beams
shining wild down trails,
skinny as hands through hair

—two figures watched boats
roll over water in gleaming
burns, shy & slow as two

snakes: one eating the mind,
the other eating

infinite flesh, some hole
in space that we name *empire*;
once we were human &

watched sunlight drape
under mountains so old
our lungs collapsed

—beyond
there is a light swaying
like a chandelier;

it passes houses along roads—
& these two—they are talking
all night, meandering into

a womb of failure, watching skulls
become clear.

IN THE BEGINNING, EVERYTHING WAS WATER

I'm not a discharge
I'm not a loss in protein
I'm not a throbbing squirm
-Sex Pistols, "Bodies"

i.

In the beginning, I was not
a man. On waters I drank
to find home, the blackest

dark. On slugs served,
I ate to understand

color, what a woman
could die from.

ii.

Do you remember when
we met? I could not say

how much I loved you.
In a waiting room,
a woman I love, who

doesn't even know me
but loves me so much—

she can't stand to keep
me like a dying
radio. She can't stand
to kill me the same way
she gave her cat to sleep.

iii.

I don't kick to calm
her down. She will think

she is making the wrong
decision if I move,
that I will come back

to haunt her when
she is older & married,
when she pulls down

a string to reveal
a bloodless tampon.

iv.

In the doctor's office,
I taste bitter

& know there is something
ugly about me. Never seen
I imagine her eating

slugs on rock salt
to satisfy me, *me*
a dash between her
and her lover, her
legs.

Inside her restless sleep,
I dream of breath.

It takes a certain kind
of skill to unfinish what
you started.

It takes a certain kind
of love to pronounce
my name, gorge

on slugs, to pull
yourself right out
of yourself.

I heard you when
 you said sorry.

LA LLORONA

We met as children:

                underwater, you pushed my head
during swim lessons. I swore to get you back.

                  Instead, you let me love you, let me hear
                            how you breathe

        when you masturbate. It's a man's world
                    but not yours when you push

        through another man. Play doctor with me
    —I can tell you where it hurts: my mouth

which asks for you, pleads for an end
        to kiss me,

    dig in dirt until we turn to wolves
ripping apart every muscle, until all we chew

                on is marrow. Our story
    is the same as others:
we married, you grew bored after three

        children, then fell in love with a bus boy.
          For the children, I kept moving

                through until I hit a wall
    & kept hitting walls
        until there were no walls. Waiting for three

            silhouettes to show
        from the wishbone

of two rivers, I wail for others to come

        —let them be wise enough to stay away.

FAMILY MOON

i.

Walls of water come in sleep. You pull sheets over your head.
In the living room, your parents sit. Football is on the television:
they say,
this is poetry. You might agree.

ii.

Red is everywhere. Is it murder, or an accident?
Doesn't matter: your hands are missing. A nail sags heavy.
This is only part of the voyage.

HEARTSTRINGS

    These buildings
                                      trap me bigger
                                                          than human
                emerge out
                                          sparkling as prosecco
                    all days pretend to be
a pearl diver / sponge
                                      soaking out its
                              family history

  Half *xenos*:
            grandmother says father's
                              side counts five times less
      as her half / on Sundays
                        this is even more true

               bread I wasn't

sacrament'd to eat
        will come back
                              buttered on right side
       haunting my left
                                  until it goes numb

  Mother only lived
                      in book pages w /

            white space

Not even thousands
                                                of flushes
                can water me out / disinfect
                                      germs reproducing
                          new germs

buy chlorinated clothes
            to stop blood
                              disease / at least thank
                  god for not giving
                        skin bluer than Lake Louise

BAINBRIDGE AVENUE

After three days of sun
Come four days of heat lightning, thunder clouds

Saola roam parking lots, horns woven
Into storm for warmth—uncharged taxi cabs

Travelled in anonymity—*schadenfreude* suburb
Not prized for their meat

Heart enjambs when abdomen rips trochee, needles shake
Trees from limbs—teeth in liver, lets out disaster

Bellies spartan of little beats: dusk in a box
Food for the rain, they slip toward extinction

THE DEVIL'S WEDDING

Say yes on the 6th
floor of a submarine;
electric eels lapping
between the pews,
singing for her mind
—boxed thunder.

White-blood shimmies
from bathroom pipes
down the aisle as she
walks, wolves in suits
claw at her ankles—
beyond the veil.

They growl & spit:
don't be naughty—
go to daddy.

UNITED STATES OF BLOOD

Mississippi River's red is low. Not enough thunderstorms
rained fat—limited cowboy fights mean no bloody steaks

for dinner. Can't find a blood diamond to buy your girl
a ring during drought. *New York Times* reports people cutting

their veins; only coffee grinds & late credit card statements
drip out. Highway signs read NEED BLOOD?

GET BLOOD HERE. Instead, red koolaid drips.
O neg & O pos went on vacay w/ B neg & A neg:

no bloodline left, only twice-removed cousins. Sirens sleep
in subway systems, slathering vaseline
on empty cockled hearts

MARY & JOSEPH BUILD A HOUSE UNDER THE BROOKLYN BRIDGE

I wanted to pull out
each other's intestines
to make guitar strings
see my hand move

around yr liver straight up
to yr lungs, stop
all breathing. For exactly

one minute, I will
extract each memory,
attach words, then
reinsert. You

will never know—it will look
like a nuclear bomb went off
in the room of yr body.

We never bothered to turn on
the lamp—only unbuckled
yr pants, hoisted off my shirt.

Behind yr mouth
is the text I want to read—
we don't speak—barely
audible moans coalescing

among white noise. 100
yrs ago, there was no
white noise, only the earth
speaking out loud.

As humans, we try
to find perfect pitch—
there's a torpedo going off
outside. It won't stop.

YOU'RE ONLY HUMAN
WHEN SOMEONE IS LOOKING

Some of the women in town
thought Mary ought to be punished.
Her belly grew to a hearse.

She prayed for a sailboat
to carry her uterus on a milk sea.
Dragonflies swarmed her flamingo-pink

plumage. She watched boys
shred guitars. May the distortion
mince all the tired women

inside her. A doctor suggested
lime in tea—an exorcise. May she
shoot wind to hear grass buzz,
to know which *she* is sprouting inside *her*.

POEMS ARE WRITTEN BY ADULTS
WHO HAVE KILLED THEIR MOTHERS

From inside
your belly, I watch

your hairs as they whiten:
this is the place
where death starts—
a well of poison

submerging half-grown
hearts imprisoning
the center of god
in sleepdeath ;;;

There must be a way out.

SIREN SONG

Were you in me, I do not know.
By morning, beta fish fought for dominance

—plucked them out, my penance not
to pray but to lose all words I love.

Yes—sea demon—swimming in my belly
reshaping woman, I flushed you down

the toilet on the river going through
a phantom spinal cord. Riding waves.

WORLD PARENT MYTH

We never repent of having eaten too little.
                                    -Thomas Jefferson

i.

Doesn't matter how it happened.
In the beginning, it started with
a woman & a piece of fruit
& a man who ate the fruit.
At the time, it was a good idea.
Hear me out—to say I was without
fear wouldn't be true /
humiliation is in all my dreams,
dreams of falling in earth.
Being sold to another.

ii.

It wasn't that I didn't love you—
I needed protecting from
my sisters & brothers / the ones
whose anger I take
because each pain means I was
alive. My first memory comes
not from your love
but theirs.

Hummed your name—
gave thanks to another
master. Whose name I didn't feel
guilty saying in bed.

Once, I remembered how
I was born—only for you
to make the worst
sacrifice: my family.

iii.

No one believed you to be
duplicitous; you never went out
in dusk. Penance was for
the rest of the world
who caused our grief /
I was never able to wear
white the way
I wanted.

Maybe you were just a man
who loved wrong
so you decided to clean
my children instead—
introduce white blood
& let purge / violence
is never far from the hands
of men.

SCIENTISTS DISCOVER HOW TO ELIMINATE EMOTION

Cloned hearts should cost 1/2
as much as real hearts when donated
—they can only feel 70% of emotion
& need to recharge every night
via lithium battery.

If left with a clone of my own heart,
will the original remember
its owner? Will lines soak out into
yr ⊠s until you throw out
yr own ⊠s?

In Dubai a woman is eaten
alive—her heart is the first to go.
The last will be her head.
Let her eat her own screams.

MARY SAID

I love forever

but not like a mother.

Name yourself for that hunger,

masturbating on your arm

until it becomes someone

else's.

SATURN RETURN

before they ate fruit
hard shells encased
their bodies
emeralds in liquor amnii

could not touch
held silence
before leaving eden
—now those shells

have retracted to finger
nails touching only
beginnings of rapture
desire's vague mentions

WE SLEEP WITH DEAD PEOPLE

We flick ashes into a Coke can
while your car drives to Queens.

Welcoming another year—we hope
to become Apollo's torso: wretchedly

human. Breath halting to a stop,
turns white. In someone's basement,

I blow you. You prefer men—
I tell you to ignore my breasts.

Millions of blood cells explode
red like pomegranate

shaving bone. Laying still we
watch as your angels uncoil—

accepting our own apokatastasis.
You come onto my breasts.

YOUR ONLY SON IS DEAD

Your only son's head
came out of water, dripping
fuchsia, Marlboro reds,
the word *fag* ;;;

boys lapped up in bodies
just like his, firebird
in reverb ;;; stole thunder
bird to bust

a town gut-jarred
—a transplant, headed
to desert: setting fire to his
bone

& watches how it
disappears, no dance
in flames—what is your
rush

MAGIC HOUR

Earth is waking from a coma
at the bottom of the lake

where your father drowned,
disrupting the fish
while we slept for eight
nights

like tangled
Christmas lights,
first breath

it's natural to be afraid
of ghosts, a man's memory,
that hour when we were
on earth alone

THE ART OF DISAPPEARING
IS HARD TO MASTER

Yesterday I rode over the George Washington
Bridge [using every inch of muscle to prevent
myself from jumping]

Water is all I know

Mother, I have not prepared myself for when
my body molts / mutates until no longer
human

Under cancer, I was born / my eyelids
so thin just scaly pupils & twilight
networking under skin

Please put me out

THE PILL VERSUS THE SPRINGHILL MINE DISASTER

for Richard Brautigan

> Don't blame me, I only killed
> what I could not take care
> of.

ONLY ASSHOLES LIVE IN BROOKLYN

We look at photographs   of French bulldogs
b/c we are bored &   it is midnight   &   we don't cry
when we're sad.

I'm here to make you lonely
in the drain of my shower   a child's heart
is clogged   like a bad decision   I swallow it.

Water drifts   my pubic hairs in a crooked
line   each hair will be shaved
never to know yr name   yr body will do

most of the work.

MITTELSCHMERZ

When getting off
the F train, I pretend to be

another woman

carrying a stroller over the gap—
in the streets, my hand falls

—as if holding another intricate
set of bones. When I'm ready,

my uterus will lunar eclipse.
You could have been

my baby. I was almost your mother.
In the gap, I left you to fall—

jarred starlight, steaming.

MY TASTE IN MEN STARTED YOUNG

i.

When I found men,
I cut my lips red, devoured skyscrapers like air.
When I pulled out
of New York

she bled months' worth of dead babies, red icicles
left in subways.

ii.

Starlings have begun to nest
elsewhere, crying me out of their hearts.
My cunt smells dirty like East River water—crows caw
until everyone's faces become mine until I burn all faces
full of faces into mosaic,

rename myself X, Witch, Other—sirens blaring
while I vomit my body out until it all suffocates,
waking to the sound of birds.

IN THE FUTURE, EVERYONE WILL FORGET WHAT THEY LOOK LIKE

        A bartender donated his organs to a casino owner
        who gambled them away & now everyone is walking

        around with a stranger's brain, cloned hearts in bones
        splintering to open sea, streaming to twenty thousand

        skulls in music notes. The echoes end in lakes—
        they are asleep as the dead insides of antelope hearts

        as a dinner no one sits down to eat. a lung fogs glass,
        echoes to a purposeless lake where another

        bartender is building a space ship to Mars.

MARYS OF THE SEA

i.

Antelopes run toward in armored florescence —
their breath the shape of faces in windowglass.
You sit & watch starlings make nests.

At one time, humans crawled on hearts greased silver
—left a trail dazzling daughters unborn, surrendering
miles. Killing them with perennials in curried fire.

Wolves follow us through subway cars, their obsession
propels them past honey bones stretched to oblivion;
bunches of lines shaped in half-circles, reaching out for us.

Ten paces away, water dragons devour emeralds
from the hands of children. Their teeth gnash
skin—blood puddles stretch into slanted metal walls.

Above ground, a paper moon wanes west—
making my slender waist more slender: empty nest.

ii.

My body wants to die but my brain can't.
Outside our building, there are cats in heat

that sound like children falling on concrete.

You roll over, fall asleep. Something above me
could have been a man. I saw *it* everyone saw *it*

& no one but me saw *it* but that's everyone
to me. Told me about a child, my child not yours.

We are two people at the bottom of a fish
tank & sometimes we recognize

each other as open/closed parentheses.

Most other times, we don't. We read
self-help books to make us passionate

because our heart valves switched off

& things feel bad on the inside now
 in new America, my America full

of everyone but me.

iii.

Inside rocks fell down subway tunnels.
The conductor has died.
Neither of us knows how to steer.
You say I remind you of ebb tides.
That I won't go away.
I tell you to get a new wife.
I'm pregnant with someone else's baby.
I don't know how it happened.
Someone told me.
I am subway tracks waiting to feel your suicide.
Just pretend I'm the child you never wanted.
Grab the next M train.
Water rushes between the walls.
Concrete holds still, for now.

iv.

Flitting between the cars is illegal
but I'm a hummingbird so it's okay
I can smell your nectar from here.

Someone is playing The Cure
way loud on their headphones.
You say you met someone else.

She's from the internet. You tell me
to go to the fish market, I'll meet
plenty of fish in the sea—

I say, it's the stench keeping
me away. A librarian hands me
a book of poetry—says it'll be my way

of staying alone. Most words
mean nothing when there's no
right font for my feelings.

v.

Looking for voices on paper
feel red all over his gummy mouth
starts to take form in my belly
hunger stops when grief replaces
my stomach lining two bodies
in one body sprouting brambles
& birds in my ears becoming deaf
to one history becoming two
histories two souls repeating
the lives of all the souls before this
one there was poetry before this
life lodged between both of us
without the dead I would lonely
be in eastern standard time
when I didn't change my name
two bodies need two names
& how does abandon form
in building how does a human
form in another human give
away another human to no one
sorceress tongue spews

spells for dead hands to throttle
what I could not inverting
empty on its head X-ray of terror
there were no repeated lives

vi.

I take this lying down.
My ragged v—you have already
forgotten me—O Father
guide my blood

to tracks where I can dump
my grief in holes. After years
of fumes I still remember
the smell of burning papers

your face in the negative
space between bush & flame
—midlight. Standing cold
outside my apt

it is still hard to imagine you
coming & going out of me
as you please. You only raped
me once, but what

portion of me died, what is still
distinguishable? So far your face
from mine—all I desire
are godlike

eyes, bigger hair to bring
me closer to heaven.

THERE IS NO G [OD] TRAIN RUNNING

You are almost human
I am already naked
You say it happened
Because you have a penis
Don't do it
I asked you nicely
Slapped the side of my face
Yr ⌧ takes away my sound
I am a new version of woman
[special features included]
I do not believe when
You push into me
I want you to be
A shotgun that shoots my cunt
Burns like brush
Now is the time baby
Laid on my back
Yr bone lights up
my palms blister
Let me hold something
Let me learn to say *sorrow*
It will stay in my mouth
Until I mean it
Push out of this body
Like a contract with yr name signed
At the end—showing off
Scarring over yr new salary
You say my heart just needed
A jump start like a Jeep Grand Cherokee
One day when you are older
You will beg
& I will breathe

THE UNIVERSE SENDS ITS CONDOLENCES

Sirens found us first.
As a defense mechanism,

my seatbelt tugged
when she was thrown

door-to-door, her heft
resting in my nose, cries

wafting around. Bodies
slackened like rotten nectarines.

There's that second after
when no one has moved

& you think, *everyone
has died around me.*

REMOVAL OF HEART ARTILLERY

                              Remembering isn't about

            how we heard

wet   towels drop on tiles,

             from the latest shower—

                      just how they kept

         falling into absence's

                                          jawbone—

listening as our

         humanity hollows us.

                      Town orchestra plays
                                 alien sex sounds
                         on late-night radio—

         towels keep falling.

                         Sister, you said, learn
                                  to speak. I unlocked
the back door: centipedes

         frothing.

IS IT THE AFTERLIFE YET?

I wrote a song
about you moving
New York into
an igloo reading
from crystal balls

giving answers
about why we won't
die in a supernova
but in Antarctica
swallowing what's left
of the titanic

sharing each of its
many hooves, light fire
to stories about birds
and mothers—mothers
and birds and bats

floating off the gulf
coast like toxic waste
with a sign that reads
please do not
swallow spoonfuls
only thimbles

& please remember
to place gauze
inside your son's
marrow to prevent
cancer that will kill
him by spring

only to release
moths belly down
on his grave, DNA
translates to speech
—now a mother
will finally know her
son's secrets:

a furnace thumps
& swans beat their
wings, gun-metal
shots melt an igloo
losing all helvetica
text.

EARTH AT THE TIME OF MERCURY RETROGRADE

i.

It was your bi-yearly crisis run. Heard your mother talk on the phone, said: another pregnancy, another marriage. Persistence isn't a key trait passed down through your family. Told me to use my name when you pushed my head under water. Bathtub flooded ears in plain sight, alphabet graphs waxing in my cavities. Just this morning, you ate oatmeal in the back patio of your apartment while a mother sat in her car across the street, newborn in the backseat.

ii.

At a certain hunger point, it is impossible to cook. In order to subdue the effects, one needs to burn sage & anoint the body with holy oil. Drink any excess oil to burn unneeded parts of the body. Cut radishes, roaches, then add snake venom into a blender. Mix until it is a thick liquid violet in color. For the next week, your body will excrete all waste, but not limited to: bullshit, ear wax, high fructose corn syrup, rage, sodium benzoate, mucus, cum, words, but most especially, rage. After this cleanse is over, how to cut a bitch in ten seconds will be second nature.

iii.

You spat three gunshots at the woman in the Toyota Corolla. It was just a breathing exorcism after all. There are 500 bats living in the house you inherited from your parents. In the master bedroom, I was gagged, 200 male-pounds of flesh hovering over my body. Lord I called out for someone who listens—some jasmine voice above me chanted and chanted. It could have been yours.

Inside me: a cat post where your penis kept clawing. Sandpaper swarming with dragonflies. In a minute, I could have been ready. In a minute where I could think of eternity's edge. In a minute, you take my neck around your fingers. Stopped my raging. I was dead but I wasn't sad. Yes, I am lying on the bed because this is where you put me & no I cannot play with you. What I say doesn't make sense anymore.

EVERYONE YOU LOVE HAS BEEN FOUND DEAD

You have not drowned.
Once in my womb, now
swarmed by waves—

grab hands say don't
love me say there are wasps
hovering say don't grab please
say it will hurt say love me, you

are different now.

PHENOMENOLOGY

Push weight of your torso
onto my face I can tell
it hurts when intestines connect
flooding tulips want to show
my legs between your legs
your ears burst tulips
uncurl demon on your left
shoulder drained twilight
swimming legless so many
wants ride through my head
bloom in your mouth's speech
no mind's eye just toss the ball
back to my court.

CHILDREN OF PARADISE (LOST)

You breath yourself:
sounds begging red / fear frequencies.

A disappearing act is hard to pull off:
hides don't hide.

Slept in your bed for
        six yrs—millipedes crawled out of my cunt

& laid their eggs
        after eating mine.

What you call your son
        is mirage.

LULLABY ON THE HALF SHELL

for W.H. Auden

Human, yr sleeping head lies
on arms with no bones.

Burn beauty away
with time. Children prove it true.

For now, lie here in my arms
our guilt entirely beautiful.

NEGATIVE SPACE

>   They both wanted her, so he proposed
>   to cut the baby in half—fair is fair.
>   How could they go home to their
>   childless husbands?
>
>   Husband gutting fish as she comes
>   back having given up her life;
>   he demands payment for her empty
>   belly. Suppose she was taken all
>
>   at once. It was better than being
>   cut in half. He combed out her jeweled
>   intestines—organ meat for dinner.
>   Out her mouth, she rose.

DEATH MASK

for William Burke

There was no one on Prince Street. In the middle
lay a skull—cement over its eyes, grotesquely

crescent frown. The skull holding breath,
a sound like typewriter keys inhabiting my body

until I peered from shut-off eyes, blind moon.
Later that week, the skull's ghost showed up

—his face sagged like a rubber chicken—dark
stains splashed down breeches.

Next to him, a woman stood, making a swinging
motion—ringing them back. I'll never walk alone

in the dark again.

WHOM ARE YOU AND WHOM DO YOU LOVE

                            In the morning you buy

                                              coffee for us

                        In yr hotel room

                                   when we make

                love

                            you never open

                                                  yr eyes

                until the end

ASSUME THE POSITION

i.

Red rosary beads the color of diluted
blood   He lies in a coffin—next
to him   I sign my name onto a sheet
of paper—the only source of   evidence
stating I exist   I am   only
three-years-old—don't know   how to
write my name

ii.

A thousand faces   I see a woman
—black beauty   I want her skin down
to the atom   I look up how to rip
particles apart on Google   Sitting
like a fat octopus   Tremont is the
next stop   [mind the gap]
afraid of tip   drill   just a girl with
ass   just a shook   one   Take
a bus to the other   side of the
country—another city   another
cluster of roads to hot wire

iii.

Play *Casta Diva* each moonrise
to sunset   Outside I can barely watch
you   the pale horse you rode on was
beheaded by a swordsman   Bite my
tongue   cross the street   Through
barred windows I see   a man making
salad   cut-up wife for dinner   Stone
wall keeps me out

At post office   I buy stamps marked
el corazon   Ask any god who is
listening to sing   hallelujah as you
jump   who does knife hits on
stoves   Watch dead stars light up
the moon   will be void tonight
Do nothing   earth shattering
There will be many delays

TAROT READING

Last night   she
        drowned

                              Rose
                                    back

up the surface
            a pelican
                              It's terrible
                    to be a bird
            when you once
had a voice
                          She is making love

                                        mute—
        he is behind
her standing
            hard as stone
                          wall, limestone-from-

        the-other-world

        He plucks her
                                        feathers

                          They grow back
He uses the others
                              as bandages
                for when she rips him up
                        for rags

            He won't have a back
                    left to stand on

```
                    She slices off the look

                                        on his face
         when she says no
                                                —touching
                        is no longer in the cards

                         If she swallows
                                    sea water
              for ten days
                     straight, an answer
                                               will appear


         Eyes see ruby            at its reddest
         turned velvet            at its softest—
                                  the planet

                         has              stopped shifting
```

Joanna C. Valente is a human who lives in Brooklyn, New York. She is the author of *Sirs & Madams* (Aldrich Press, 2014), *The Gods Are Dead* (Deadly Chaps Press, 2015), *Marys of the Sea*, & *Xenos* (forthcoming 2017, Agape Editions). She received her MFA in writing at Sarah Lawrence College. She is also the founder of *Yes, Poetry*, as well as the managing editor for *Luna Luna Magazine*. Some of her writing has appeared in *Prelude, The Atlas Review, The Feminist Wire, BUST, Pouch*, and elsewhere. She also teaches workshops at Brooklyn Poets.

POETICS AND PROCESS

*Joanna C. Valente in conversation
with Lynne DeSilva-Johnson*

Who are you?

Joanna C. Valente, a human, alien, sea creature, or ghost.

Why are you a poet?

Because poetry is honest. Because poetry mimicks the rhythm of the heart and the fragmented way the brain thinks.

When did you decide you were a poet (and/or: do you feel comfortable calling yourself a poet, what other titles or affiliations do you prefer/feel are more accurate)?

I began writing when I was 11, and while I didn't consider myself a poet, I also took writing seriously even then. I was a pretty serious kid and had been painting and drawing since I could remember, so in many ways, it's also accurate to generally say I am an artist—and have been for most, if not all, of my life in various ways and forms. Thinking analytically and yearning to find the meaning in the stories I tell, the stories of my life and others', has always been important to me, because it helps us understand the world around us. And hopefully, that makes us kinder and more compassionate.

What's a "poet", anyway?

A poet is a type of prophet, telling us how we feel, what the world is evolving into, what our hidden desires and sadnesses are.

What is the role of the poet today?

I believe poets are activists, and should be advocating for progressive positive change, to create a freer and more inclusive world where everyone is valued—where we are able to build safe lives for ourselves. Where we can openly feel.

What do you see as your cultural and social role (in the poetry community and beyond)?

For me, I want to be a supportive and compassionate person, an advocate for those around me who are driven by their own beliefs and truths—and connect others through my art and writing. In general, I am always working toward creating more awareness about sexual assault and sexual violence, and want to create a space for survivors to come forward and feel seen—and to feel as if we are creating a world where sexual violence is not tolerated or excused.

Talk about the process or instinct to move these poems (or your work in general) as independent entities into a body of work. How and why did this happen? Have you had this intention for a while? What encouraged and/or confounded this (or a book, in general) coming together? Was it a struggle?

Each poem is like a child to me—they are at once something I birth into the world—but they also take on lives of their own, through the meanings others interpret through them. In general, I also look at each poem as being their own microcosm within the larger collection or world they inhabit. Each poem has a unique POV and persona that speaks to larger issues, like gender and sexual identity.

This particular book, for instance, was a way for me to explore my sexual assault and subsequent abortion I had because of it, as a way to achieve understanding of what happened to me, of what happened to my body—and let it go, like a spell. I began writing the book as my MFA thesis while at Sarah Lawrence College. And while the book was a struggle, to relive these moments and memories, it was also cathartic. I used the trope of Mother Mary/Mary Magadalene to tell the story, but also comment on sexual and gender identity, and what it means to be both in control and powerless over one's own body—to have multuple identities and dualities.

Did you envision this collection as a collection or understand your process as writing specifically around a theme while the poems themselves were being written? How or how not?

I always envisioned it as being an entire collection, as I wanted to tell a story—and to do that, you need time and space in order to create a narrative that not only makes sense to the reader, but is rich and nuanced enough to hold them. While I wrote in the Marys persona, it was also largely about me—which made it easier to write as I was writing around my experiences.

What formal structures or other constrictive practices (if any) do you use in the creation of your work?

At the time, I was very interested in using the entire space on the page and experimenting with line breaks, punctuation, and indentation—so I was often taking myself out of my comfort zone and trying to find new ways to use the negative spaces on the page—because poetry is like a painting, as the page is the canvas and the poem is the image.

Have certain teachers or instructive environments, or readings/writings of other creative people (poets or others) informed the way you work/write?

Of course. Everyone I encounter does. I believe every moment influences me. Being in workshops since I was an undergraduate definitely has influenced me, as I was able to understand the difference between what I see on the page and what my reader does—and how to tell a story through poetry. I also believe the workshop environment stressed to me just how much editing is a part of writing. Some influences include Monica Ferrell, Cathy Park Hong, Marie Howe, and many others.

Speaking of monikers, what does your title represent? How was it generated? Talk about the way you titled the book, and how your process of naming (poems, sections, etc) influences you and/or colors your work specifically.

The title represents the dualities that exist within one's own sexual and gender identity—while also implying a disconnect as well. Marys of the Sea encompasses the Mother Mary/Mary Magdalene personas, while also illustrating the many identities (and fluid identities) we have. The title actually is a Tori Amos song as well, and Tori Amos is definitely, and has always been, an influence on me.

What does this particular collection of poems represent to you
…as indicative of your method/creative practice?
…as indicative of your history?
…as indicative of your mission/intentions/hopes/plans?

Historically, the collection is largely about sexual assault and abortion, which represents experiences that have personally shaped my life—and experiences I hope that help other survivors cope with their own experiences. And make them feel less alone, most of all. In general, I like to experiment and push myself, and the structure of these poems definitely reflect that.

What does this book DO (as much as what it says or contains)?

It challenges the status quo, how we see our bodies within society, and how to fight against those boundaries.

What would be the best possible outcome for this book? What might it do in the world, and how will its presence as an object facilitate your creative role in your community and beyond? What are your hopes for this book, and for your practice?

I hope it helps others feel less alone if they feel like they don't fit a mold, if they have experienced traumas, and allow others to write about their traumas and experiences honestly and boldly.

Let's talk a little bit about the role of poetics and creative community in social activism, in particular in what I call "Civil Rights 2.0," which has remained immediately present all around us in the time leading up to this series' publication. I'd be curious to hear some thoughts on the challenges we face in speaking and publishing across lines of race, age, privilege, social/cultural background, and sexuality within the community, vs. the dangers of remaining and producing in isolated "silos."

Right now, we face serious inequalities across race, gender, sexuality, and privilege when it comes to publishing. Often times, I do feel the publishing world is afraid to make bold statements, and often goes with the status-quo, or what is deemed as most sellable, so to speak. I think this is dangerous. In general, it dangerous to attach money to art, and put the most value on what makes the most money—because that doesn't, of course, necessarily translate to what is actually the most honest, influential, and brave—or diverse. Diversity of voices and experience (for instance, people of color and people with special needs/disabilities) are often left out, because it only appeals to a "certain audience." There are some presses, big and small, putting out provactive and groundbreaking work, but I do feel like there aren't enough.

This, in turn, results in smaller indie presses taking the real risks and putting out the type of work that I believe is groundbreaking and authentic—however, this usually means people finding out about these books are within that specific lit community—meaning that the work is isolated to that community. That in itself is dangerous, because it means slower change, slower activism (even if it doesn't always feel that way because of the internet).

WHY PRINT / DOCUMENT?

The Operating System uses the language "print document" to differentiate from the book-object as part of our mission to distinguish the act of documentation-in-book-FORM from the act of publishing as a backwards facing replication of the book's agentive *role* as it may have appeared the last several centuries of its history. Ultimately, I approach the book as TECHNOLOGY: one of a variety of printed documents (in this case bound) that humans have invented and in turn used to archive and disseminate ideas, beliefs, stories, and other evidence of production.

Ownership and use of printing presses and access to (or restriction of printed materials has long been a site of struggle, related in many ways to revolutionary activity and the fight for civil rights and free speech all over the world. While (in many countries) the contemporary quotidian landscape has indeed drastically shifted in its access to platforms for sharing information and in the widespread ability to "publish" digitally, even with extremely limited resources, the importance of publication on physical media has not diminished. In fact, this may be the most critical time in recent history for activist groups, artists, and others to insist upon learning, establishing, and encouraging personal and community documentation practices. Hear me out.

With The OS's print endeavors I wanted to open up a conversation about this: the ultimately radical, transgressive act of creating PRINT /DOCUMENTATION in the digital age. It's a question of the archive, and of history: who gets to tell the story, and what evidence of our life, our behaviors, our experiences are we leaving behind? We can know little to nothing about the future into which we're leaving an unprecedentedly digital document trail — but we can be assured that publications, government agencies, museums, schools, and other institutional powers that be will continue to leave BOTH a digital and print version of their production for the official record. Will we?

As a (rogue) anthropologist and long time academic, I can easy pull up many accounts about how lives, behaviors, experiences — how THE STORY of a time or place — was pieced together using the deep study of correspondence, notebooks, and other physical documents which are no longer the norm in many lives and practices. As we move our creative behaviors towards digital note taking, and even audio and video, what can we predict about future technology that is in any way assuring that our stories will be accurately told – or told at all? How will we leave these things for the record?

In these documents we say:
WE WERE HERE, WE EXISTED, WE HAVE A DIFFERENT STORY

- Lynne DeSilva-Johnson, Founder/Managing Editor,
THE OPERATING SYSTEM, Brooklyn NY 2017

TITLES IN THE FEINER DOCUMENT COLLECTION

An Absence So Great and Spontaneous It Is Evidence of Light - Anne Gorrick [2018]
Chlorosis   - Michael Flatt and Derrick Mund [2018]
Sussuros a Mi Padre - Erick Sáenz [2018]
Jazzercise is a Language - Gabriel Ojeda-Sague [2018]
Death is a Festival - Anis Shivani [2018]
Return Trip / Viaje Al Regreso; Dual Language Edition - Israel Dominguez,(trans. Margaret Randall) [2018]
Born Again - Ivy Johnson [2018]
Singing for Nothing - Wally Swist [2018]

One More Revolution - Andrea Mazzariello [2017]
Fugue State Beach - Filip Marinovich [2017]
Lost City Hydrothermal Field - Peter Milne Greiner [2017]
The Book of Everyday Instruction - Chloe Bass [2017]
In Corpore Sano : Creative Practice and the Challenged Body [Anthology, 2017] Lynne DeSilva-Johnson and Jay Besemer, co-editors
Love, Robot - Margaret Rhee[2017]
The Furies - William Considine [2017]
Nothing Is Wasted - Shabnam Piryaei [2017]
Mary of the Seas - Joanna C. Valente [2017]
You Look Something - Jessica Tyner Mehta [2017]
CHAPBOOK SERIES 2017 : INCANTATIONS
featuring original cover art by Barbara Byers
sp. - Susan Charkes; Radio Poems - Jeffrey Cyphers Wright; Fixing a Witch/Hexing the Stitch - Jacklyn Janeksela; cosmos a personal voyage by carl sagan ann druyan steven sotor and me - Connie Mae Oliver
Flower World Variations, Expanded Edition/Reissue - Jerome Rothenberg and Harold Cohen [2017]
Island - Tom Haviv [2017]
What the Werewolf Told Them / Lo Que Les Dijo El Licantropo - Chely Lima (trans. Margaret Randall) [2017]
The Color She Gave Gravity - Stephanie Heit [2017]
The Science of Things Familiar - Johnny Damm [Graphic Hybrid, 2017]
agon - Judith Goldman [2017]
To Have Been There Then / Estar Alli Entonces - Gregory Randall (trans. Margaret Randall) [2017]

Instructions Within - Ashraf Fayadh [2016]
Arabic-English dual language edition; Mona Kareem, translator
Let it Die Hungry - Caits Meissner [2016]
A GUN SHOW - Adam Sliwinski and Lynne DeSilva-Johnson;
So Percussion in Performance with Ain Gordon and Emily Johnson [2016]
Everybody's Automat [2016] - Mark Gurarie
How to Survive the Coming Collapse of Civilization [2016] - Sparrow
CHAPBOOK SERIES 2016: OF SOUND MIND
*featuring the quilt drawings of Daphne Taylor
Improper Maps - Alex Crowley; While Listening - Alaina Ferris;
Chords - Peter Longofono; Any Seam or Needlework - Stanford Cheung

TEN FOUR - Poems, Translations, Variations [2015]- Jerome Rothenberg, Ariel Resnikoff, Mikhl Likht
MARILYN [2015] - Amanda Ngoho Reavey
CHAPBOOK SERIES 2015: OF SYSTEMS OF
*featuring original cover art by Emma Steinkraus
Cyclorama - Davy Knittle; The Sensitive Boy Slumber Party Manifesto - Joseph Cuillier; Neptune Court - Anton Yakovlev; Schema - Anurak Saelow
SAY/MIRROR [2015; 2nd edition 2016] - JP HOWARD
Moons Of Jupiter/Tales From The Schminke Tub [plays, 2014] - Steve Danziger

CHAPBOOK SERIES 2014: BY HAND
Pull, A Ballad - Maryam Parhizkar; Can You See that Sound - Jeff Musillo
Executive Producer Chris Carter - Peter Milne Grenier;
Spooky Action at a Distance - Gregory Crosby;

CHAPBOOK SERIES 2013: WOODBLOCK
*featuring original prints from Kevin William Reed
Strange Coherence - Bill Considine; The Sword of Things - Tony Hoffman; Talk About Man Proof - Lancelot Runge / John Kropa; An Admission as a Warning Against the Value of Our Conclusions -Alexis Quinlan

DOC U MENT
/däkyəmənt/

First meant "instruction" or "evidence," whether written or not.

noun - a piece of written, printed, or electronic matter that provides information or evidence or that serves as an official record
verb - record (something) in written, photographic, or other form
synonyms - paper - deed - record - writing - act - instrument

[*Middle English, precept, from Old French, from Latin documentum, example, proof, from docre, to teach; see dek- in Indo-European roots.*]

Who is responsible for the manufacture of value?

Based on what supercilious ontology have we landed in a space where we vie against other creative people in vain pursuit of the fleeting credibilities of the scarcity economy, rather than freely collaborating and sharing openly with each other in ecstatic celebration of MAKING?

While we understand and acknowledge the economic pressures and fear-mongering that threatens to dominate and crush the creative impulse, we also believe that **now more than ever we have the tools to relinquish agency via cooperative means,** fueled by the fires of the Open Source Movement.

Looking out across the invisible vistas of that rhizomatic parallel country we can begin to see our community beyond constraints, in the place where intention meets resilient, proactive, collaborative organization.

Here is a document born of that belief, sown purely of imagination and will.

When we document we assert.

We print to make real, to reify our being there.
When we do so with mindful intention to address our process,
to open our work to others, to create beauty in words in space,
to respect and acknowledge the strength of the page we now hold physical,
a thing in our hand… we remind ourselves that, like Dorothy:
we had the power all along, my dears.

THE PRINT! DOCUMENT SERIES

is a project of
the trouble with bartleby
in collaboration with
the operating system

www.ingramcontent.com/pod-product-compliance
Lightning Source LLC
Chambersburg PA
CBHW021447080526
44588CB00009B/725